Marketing Your Small Business Online
Using the Web to Snare more Customers

By Terry C Power

www.GreensboroOnlineMarketing.com

Dedication

This work is dedicated to all the small business owners and entrepreneurs who drive our economy. I'm proud to say this group included my father. Also a big thanks to my family. And good friends like Myrym.

And especially to Lynne, my best friend and the true love of my life. Thank you for everything.

Contents

What we'll learn

Throughout this book I'm going to cover how you can increase your profits by capitalizing on the power of the world wide web. I'll cover several techniques you can implement on your own and some you'd probably be better off hiring out. Many business owners are hesitant to start marketing their business online because they do not understand what it involves and simply overwhelmed with the whole concept. Once you understand the basics of what goes into marketing online, it is just a matter of taking action in order to succeed.

I'll be covering what to do if you don't have a website and what to do oce you have one. Many of the techniques do not require a website but will work with one also.

I suggest reading a chapter then considering how you can implement that particular strategy then either begin using the technique or at least plan how you will use it before moving to the following chapter. This will allow you to immediately began capitalizing on the immense power of the Internet and each step builds your web presence stronger.

So without further ado let's begin with the question I hear most often from local business owners,

"Do I need a website ?"

Do you need a website ?

Do you have a business ? Would you like customers to call you ? Want them to come to your door ? Want to increase profits while lowering ad costs ? Then, YES, you need a website!
Why do you need an online presence? You need an active online salesman working for you, bringing customers to you and telling potential customers how you can provide the solution to their problem. And doing all of this while you are busy with other customers or running your business.

" 2. 2 billion local business searches occurred in December 2008. 82% of Local Searchers follow-up offline via an in-store visit, phone call, or purchase, emphasizing the importance for companies to integrate their on-and offline information." -
(comScore for TMP Directional Marketing, August 2009)

A good website tells people what you offer them, where you are and how they can contact you or talk with you and ask you questions. It also allows you to answer their questions and anticipate their needs as well as showing both your expertise and your enthusiasm for your product or service. It should be a two way conversation between your business and potential customers.

The first sources that Americans turn to for local business information are search engines (31%), print Yellow Pages or White Pages (30%), internet Yellow Pages (IYP) sites (19%) and local search sites (11%). –
(Local Search Usage Study: TMP Directional Marketing, conducted by comScore, 2009)

This is the 21st century so you do need a website, but you can begin to leverage the web before your site is developed. Later on we'll discuss what you want in a website and why, but we'll begin with some techniques you can use before and after you have a website.

Let's go !

An online marketing primer

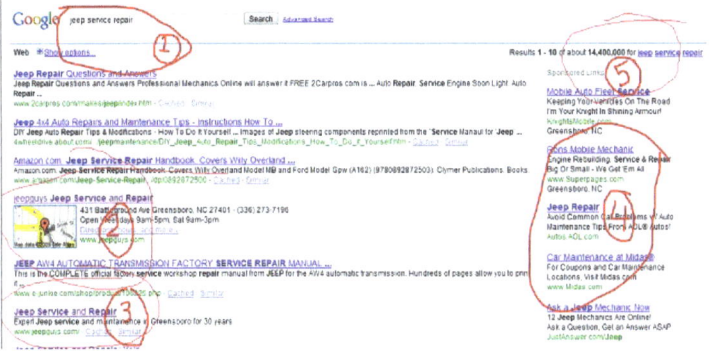

figure 1

Figure 1 above shows the search results page when I did a search for the words " jeep service repair ". The above picture is from a search on Google.com Google is a search engine, in fact the most popular search engine in the U.S. While there are other search engines they all serve the common purpose of helping us find things we are seeking. And as business owners, we want people who are seeking something we offer to find us before our competitors.

In the example above I've circled some objects of which you should be aware. **Number one** is our " keyword " or the term someone types in when searching. Staying with this example, if someone is looking to buy a new jeep they would most likely not put in the words "service" or "repair" but perhaps "dealer" or "sales".

The important message here is that you want to be found by those who would be good customers for you, i.e. someone looking for a new Jeep might not be the ideal customer for an auto mechanic. Give some thought to what "keywords" your potential customers might use.

Number two above is a " local business listing " and Google (and other search engines) offers these listings to business owners at no cost !! We'll cover how to claim your listings shortly.

Number three is an organic listing. This simply means that the search engine found this web page while looking for pages relevant to the "keyword" that was typed in. Note that search engines list web pages not websites which can be an important consideration. Ten organic listings appear on the first page and being on that page is nearly essential for successful online marketing.

Number four are paid listings and as the term implies, someone is paying to have their ads appear there. The cost depends on the keyword they've chosen and they are charged every time someone clicks on their ad. I'm not recommending this but many have hurt their competition by clicking on their ads and thereby costing them money. These PPC (pay Per Click) campaigns can be effective but can also be expensive if not done properly.

Number five on the figure is the number of web pages found that are competing for the keyword " jeep service repair ". In this case, there are over 14 million web pages so getting on the first page can be challenging. But ten of them have done it.

One other term of importance is Domain name or URL. In the figure above you can see the domain names in green. In the item circled number three, the URL or domain name is www.JeepGuys.com Most domain names have some connection to the information on the website it is associated with and your domain name should be indicative of what you do or where you are or ideally both.

For those who are curious URL stands for Universal Resource Locator which just means a domain name makes it easier to find your website than a string of numbers which is actually what the computers are using. A domain name such as ClevelandChiropractic.com or BoiseBasketMakers.com is preferable to SamJohnston.com or Orvilles.com because we want customers who are unfamiliar with us to find us as easily as our current customers having a URL that incorporates the keywords for our business is very helpful. .

Ok, now that you've given some thought to your domain name and you understand keywords, lets get started getting your business listed online !

First things first

Email addresses .

Get email addresses in the name of your business.
Like
ClevelandChiropractic@gmail.com or
BoiseBasketMakers@yahoo.com
Go to Google and sign up for a Gmail account in
the name of your business and get a similar
Hotmail account and then a Yahoo account. These
three e-mail addresses will allow you to post
business listings on the search engines.

Got Them ? OK.

Getting your business listed.

Alright now that you've signed up for the three e-mail accounts we're ready to put your business on the search engines. Go to www.GetListed.org and type in the name your business and the location then hit the enter key.

  On the right side of the screen you'll see where you can put your business on each of the search engines listed. This is why you need the email addresses.

 You'll need to go to the following pages:

Google Local Business Center
http://www.google.com/local/add

Yahoo
http://listings.local.yahoo.com/signup/create_1.php

Microsoft Bing
https://ssl.bing.com/listings/ListingCenter.aspx

Once again, since they are the dominant search engine, we'll use Google for our example of how best to utilize these business listings.

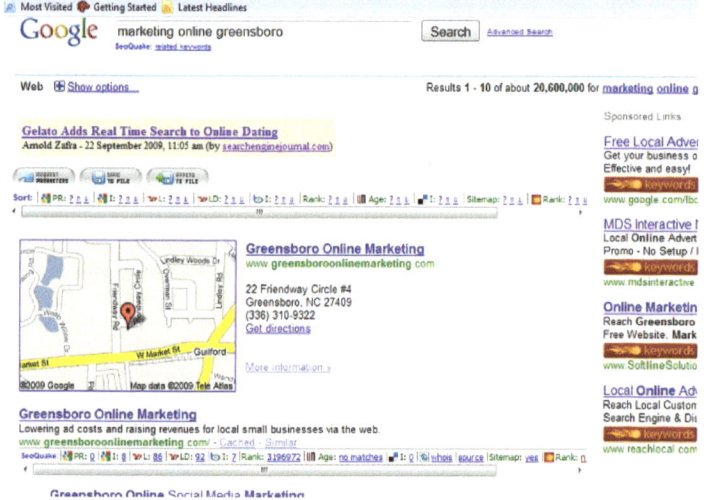

Figure 2

Figure 2 shows a finished Google business center listing or maps listing. These normally show up on Google's first page and if done properly can bring amazing response rates. Note in figure 2 that my maps listing shows on the first page out of over 20 million competing web pages and even above my organic listings !

How to get the most out of a local maps listing
http://www.google.com/local/add/businessCenter

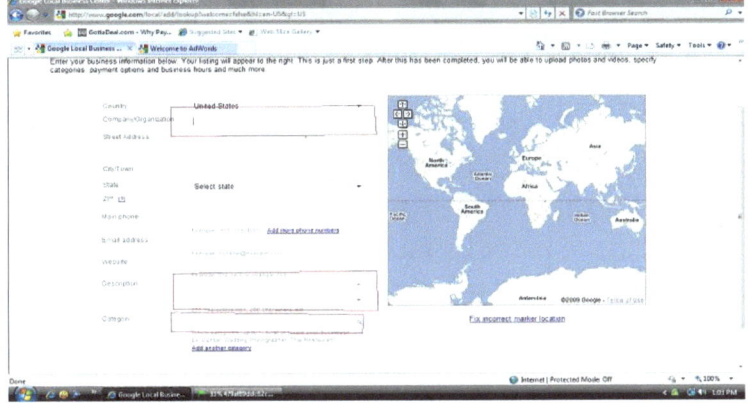

First we'll begin with the first box. Remember your"keywords" ? We want to use those in this box followed by the company name, such as "Jonesboro Septic Cleaning – Don's Septic service" or "Miami Accountant – Jorge Martinez, CPA"
After this fill in your info making certain the phone number you enter is your business phone. When we get to the "Description" we again focus on your "keywords". For instance,
" Jonesboro septic cleaning has been the specialty of Don's Septic Service for the last 12 years. Regular maintenance and septic cleaning should not be ignored. If you're in the Jonesboro area and need septic cleaning, call Don's. "
Be creative but try to get your keywords in there twice if possible.

When you fill in the "Category" box, Google offers some choices and you can accept them or not. You have the option (so use it !) of entering this listing in up to 5 categories. Use Google's suggestion in at least one of those 5. After clicking "Submit" you're brought to another page where you have the option of adding more information.

I recommend using as much of these as possible. Add a photo of your storefront or yourself. A testimonial video of a satisfied customer or client. Specify your hours and days of operation. There is room for "additional info" (Google suggests mentioning parking availability or other extras you offer) but consider this another opportunity to use those "keywords" you by now have memorized.

For instance,

"Jonesboro Septic Cleaning   Septic Repairs
Septic Installation   Septic Maintenance "

When you hit the "Submit" key you'll be asked to verify the listing. Use the phone method rather than waiting weeks on Google. You'll get a call from Google's robot which will give you a four or five digit code you need to enter as your PIN.

Once that is completed you're done !

(now go get started on Yahoo and Bing)

Within 48 hours your listing should appear on Google when anyone searches using your "keywords". You can go back into Google's Local Business Center and edit your listing as needed by signing in to your Gmail account and going to settings.

On the following page you'll find a list of 30+ directories to which you can add your business.

Get ready for that phone to start ringing!

More Business Listing Sites

1. 6Qube Directory
2. AdTurtle.com
3. Anepedia.com
4. Best of the Web
Follow this link -
http://local.botw.org/helpcenter/jumpstartpr
oduct.aspx to create a free
"Jump Start" business listing.
5. BizHWY
6. BizJournals
7. Brownbook.net
8. CitySlick.net
9. GenieKnows
10. GetFreeListing.com
11. GoMyLocal.com
12. HotFrog.com
13. HowEarlyToday.com
14. HowLateToday.com
15. infoUSA.com
16. Jadyn Ave.
17. JustClickLocal
18. localD.com19. LocalDatabase
20. LocalPages.com
21. Yelp
22. LocalRollCall
23. LymaBean.com
24. Matchpoint

25. Merchant Circle
26. NitPickIt Local Business Listings
27. Outside.in
28. Qxiu Business Directory
29. Topix.net
30. Town USA
31. CheckMyReviews.com
32. CitySquares
33. Cylex
34. InsiderPages.com
35. MojoPages.com
36. Yellow Assistance
37. YellowBot

That ought to get you some notice !

Testimonials

Since, in reality, all business is about relationships, let's discuss some ways to help the potential customer come to know, like and trust you as the one with the solution to their problem. You should let your customers know they are valued and you can do this while simultaneously telling potential new customers that your product or service is valuable to them and others. We do this by way of testimonials. Testimonials are a great way to give your potential customers the confidence to know that they are working with someone that they can trust. If you haven't put some great testimonials on your site, you need to do it now. Unless you are a Fortune 5,000 company, chances are that first time visitors to your site have no way of knowing how well you will respond to their needs.

I can tell you my service is great, that my customers love my products and services, that people will be talking about GreensboroOnlineMarketing for years to come. But coming from me, most anything that I say will sound like arrogance.

In order to be effective, testimonials need to be good. Here's an example of a poor testimonial:
===============

"I love your service !" - Anonymous

What's wrong with loving my service ? Nothing! But, notice that it doesn't really tell you why my service is so
great and it doesn't tell you who thinks it's great either!
In order to be effective testimonials need to be specific
and we need to have the confidence that a real person made those comments.
How about this example?
================

"I am an amateur artist who recently ordered your Artist's Best easel. I just had to write and let you know how satisfied I am with your product! The wood, finish and craftsmanship on my easel was superb. It was shipped sooner than I expected and putting it together was not really difficult.
I honestly thought that I would never be able to afford my own easel. It is always a little scary ordering over the Internet from companies that are not known to you, but I am so glad that I took a chance on you!"
Wilma Bellows, Melbourne, FL

  This person is only "satisfied" but, notice how much more personal this testimonial is. The customer talks about the fears that we all have and the way that it worked out for her.The good news is, that if you know how to do it, getting quality testimonials isn't anywhere near as hard as most of you would think.

The hidden secret that somehow seems to elude most business owners when getting testimonials is really very simple, just ask.

Send your existing customers an email and let them know that their opinions are important to you. Ask them to give you some specific examples of ways that your company has helped them in their life or business.

One more thing! Offer to post links to their site directly from their testimonial if you use it on your website. They will get extra traffic to their site just for telling the truth about their experience with your company!

Here's a sample email for generating some testimonials:

===============

"Just a quick note to ask your help. I'm currently looking for some great "specific" testimonials to put up on our various web sites from customers like yourself. It would be great if you could take just a second to hit the reply button and type in a few lines to tell me about something that I did for you as a customer that was helpful or something that you like about our products and services that I could share with the visitors to my web sites. If you are willing to share your experience with me, I will post the best ones to my web sites along with a link to your web site. Hopefully, that will generate extra traffic for your site and help me give potential customers the confidence that they need to become part of the GreensboroOnlineMarketing family of customers."

To top it all off, you will get a lot of very
nice comments about you that just may
make your day!
As an example, here are a couple of actual
testimonials I got by sending the above email.

*"I knew very little about the tools that are available to
optimize my website visibility. I met with Terry from
GreensboroOnlineMarketing, who is very professional
and obviously knowledgeable in his area of expertise, yet
he has an uncanny ability to explain things in layman's
terms for people like me, so that I could actually put his
advice into use. If someone doesn't know of your website,
and they can't otherwise find you using search engines,
I've no doubt that Terry can make a noticeable difference"*
Natalie S
www.time4yourlifenow.com

*"Terry was very instrumental in assisting me getting
my
business website up and running. He took the time to
meet me and was very patient with explaining exactly
what I needed to do and also to increase the exposure
of
my website. He is knowledgeable and very courteous.
Thanks for all your help!"*
-Leslie R

These kind words help make the current customers feel good to know you want their opinions, they make you feel good to be reminded that your service is appreciated and most importantly, they assure potential new customers that yours is a reputable and respected business whose customers are looked after. Something as simple as a follow up with a customer can lead to these glowing testimnials and also reminds the customer that it was a good experience and by keeping it in the forefront of their mind you may get repeat business from them or some good referrals as they mention to friends or coworkers that you cared enough to follow up with them.

Never underestimate the value of relationships.

Email Marketing

Get your customers' email addresses. They can be a valuable asset that can pay you dividends for years. Ask for them when someone contacts you and have a place in your business where they can enter their email in exchange for a discount on their next purchase or for information on future specials, etc... Offer them something for this information and follow through. E-mail lists can enable you to generate awareness and, more importantly, build mutually beneficial relationships with key audiences.

You can quickly and easily set up mailing lists using Microsoft Outlook or Outlook Express, Eudora, Yahoo, Hotmail and other popular e-mail software and services. It's simply a matter of following the instructions provided. If you envision creating larger lists or prefer not to deal with administrative tasks such as removing bad e-mail addresses and manually adding new people to the list, consider services such as bCentral List Builder, Yahoo! Groups, and Topica. These services enable you to set up and oversee mailing lists quickly and easily.

It's a relatively simple task to set up a mailing list, regardless of which option you choose. But more must be done to get the most benefit from your list.

Begin by answering the following questions.

What's the purpose of the mailing list?

First, decide whether you have worthwhile information to communicate. Second, determine whether e-mail is the best tool for communicating this information.

Who is the audience for the mailing list?

Customers? Vendors? Business partners? Media?

An effective mailing list -- or any form of communication, for that matter – can't meet the needs of all audiences. You need to focus your content to have a chance at succeeding in your communications efforts.

What content will you offer, and how will you present it?
You not only need to determine what to include on your list but how often you will disseminate information, where to get it, and how to present it in a format suitable for email. In other words, you'll have to develop a schedule for collecting, developing and formatting mailing list content. You'll need to consider offering mailing list subscribers options for how they want to receive information,

as plain text or as an HTML document.

How will the list be promoted?

The possibilities are endless. You can mention it on your Web site, in your signature file, on your letterhead and packaging, and in any other communication directed at your target audience: e-mail, brochures, business cards, press releases, articles and voice mail.

Will the list be used for announcements or discussion?
You can use a mailing list to send press releases, product details and other materials to subscribers without offering them the option of contributing to the list content or talking to each other. These lists are often referred to as announcement or distribution lists. Imagine being able to turn your slow period into a busy period simply emailing your list and offering a 7% discount on Tuesdays for instance, or turning smaller profit customers into larger ones by mailing your list an offer of 15% off multiple orders or the like. By being able to keep in touch, you can more effectively advertise to them.
However, you might wish to create a discussion list that allows subscribers to exchange ideas.

This alternative might be attractive if the list consists of individuals for whom the ability to interact with colleagues is essential. Mailing lists used for discussion purposes typically demand more active management. Such mailing lists tend to suffer when members send incendiary messages or when they fail to stay on topic or otherwise don't contribute constructively and substantively. Skillful list management creates a supportive, productive environment. Be sure to consider the ongoing commitment this role requires when allocating resources to Internet public relations activities.

Is membership in the list open to anyone, or is it restricted? You might wish to allow anyone interested in a list to subscribe to it. But some lists, such as those just for customers, will be exclusive, so you'll need to evaluate each request to join. Again, such a task adds to the work of managing the mailing list.

Will the list be moderated? A mailing list moderator plays the role of traffic cop, receiving messages subscribers want to post to the list and determining whether they are appropriate. This role allows you to remain tuned in to what's important to your subscribers and to build relationships through the conversation.

The alternative is to create an unmoderated list.

You might also wish to create a searchable archive of all mailing list content, which benefits current as well as prospective members.

Once you've got the ball rolling, follow these guidelines:

•**Be concise.** Write in short paragraphs and provide summaries of longer articles. Include links to additional information for those who want it.

•**Create a welcome message** that is immediately sent to subscribers. This message should include the list's purpose and target audience, frequency, appropriate topics for submissions, and contacts for questions about list content and technical issues.

•**Create an opt-in mailing list**, whereby you invite people to subscribe - rather than simply adding them without notice. It's to your distinct advantage to send information only to subscribers who have chosen to receive it, rather than alienating people you've added indiscriminately.

•**Make it easy to subscribe and unsubscribe** from your lists. Always include information on how to subscribe and unsubscribe at the end of all mailing list messages. Subscribers often don't save or can't easily find your introductory message that includes list directions.

Or,hopefully, they've forwarded the message to someone who's not currently a subscriber but who decides to join.

•**Assure subscribers** that their e-mail addresses will not be sold or used for any purpose other than list-related communication.

•**Be true** to your purpose, audience and content. In other words, give your subscribers what you promised and, presumably, what they value.

The Internet is overflowing with mailing lists clamoring for subscribers. By following these guidelines, you'll stand out, attract a loyal following of subscribers, and be on the way to creating a list that meets your public relations goals.

Done right email marketing to a list can be an effective and efficient means of retaining customers and bringing in new ones.

Building relationships builds businesses

Do you Twitter ?
Social Media and Your Business

Social Media sites are exploding all over the internet. Ever since internet marketers became conscious of how beneficial they can be to broaden their customer base, these networking sites have started to become popular among more than just those interested in chatting with online friends.

It is now known as a powerful marketing tool for online businesses.

What is social media or Social Networking?...

Social Networking is an online community of like-minded people looking to link up with those who share the same interests. These people connect together in a web-based area to share information, tips, share experiences or just chat about themselves. The websites that provide these networking services are known as Social Media sites and they either specialize in one group of people, like those looking for local friendships, or they provide a service where you can start your own community of cyber friends to network with.

How can this benefit YOUR business?

Social networking sites have been one of the best marketing tools online businesses have used. Most of the successful online business owners agree that this way of advertising should be in your marketing arsenal of tools. Here's why they believe that no one should leave this stone unturned:

Low-cost-
This marketing tool can save you quite a lot of money by giving you a route to learn all about your customers. You can find out what they like, dislike and what problems they frequently face. Once you find out what your potential customers want, you can create those products to give them what they're looking for.

Building Trust-
These networking sites give you the ability to connect with your customers and build rapport with them. You start to gain trust and credibility with them as they get to know you in a more personal, socializing manner. Your website is your business card, but it doesn't give your target audience a sense for who you really are. Connecting with them on a social level gives them that face to the name mentality.

Gain contacts-
You would be surprised at all the people you could ultimately be connecting with. Those contacts can help find other customers or even more effective products to use or sell in your business. Keep in mind, each person you meet- knows other people who know other people and so on. All those people could find their way to your site to buy your items or use your service.

Educational-
You can learn new things about the topic your website provides. Others who are interested in the same topic can broaden your horizons and teach you things you didn't know before or show you where to get more resources on the subject. Reciprocate the favor they extend to you and they may be even more helpful in the future.

Increases your site ranks-
Social networking sites allow you to have inbound links to your website. Not only can you drive more traffic to that site from others in the community, but you can also increase your rankings in the search engines. They like inbound links provided they relate to each other. Those inbound links can become link bait, which allows others to link to it as well, which gives you a broader visitor base. Your site visitor numbers can rise quickly.

Building a Brand-
If your business has a brand, these networking sites are great ways to make your potential customers and their friends more aware of your brand and your company. Brand awareness helps people remember your site and not your competitors when they need to buy an item that you're offering.

Keep up to date-
This is one of the easiest ways to keep up to date on what's going on within the internet. If there are new tools to use for your business, new products to try or even new items that your customers are searching for, you will more than likely find them here. With a whole scope of people to connect with, someone somewhere will probably know something you don't.

Sell your products or services-
Once you join a community and get to know you're community members well, you can start selling your items. Reciprocate the favors by purchasing what they have and they may be willing to start referring their customers to your website business.

Joint venture partnerships-
Some joint partnerships were started when some members of social networking sites worked out a deal to combine their efforts and sell a certain product. By combining those items, you're providing a more desirable product that could be sold for more money.

Inexpensive-
Most of these sites are free to join and easy to sign up with. It only takes a little time and effort on your part to get your profile set up and get your "space" created and ;you're then on your way to socializing, networking and eventually building a bigger customer base.

Some things to remember when social networking

Social Networking sites are great marketing tools to use to reach hundreds or even thousands of people, in some cases. They're easy to use and sometimes are quick to bring results; but they shouldn't be taken too lightly.

Here are some things to remember when using one of these sites for your business:

Use your real name-
Since you're trying to build some credibility and trust with potential customers, you will want to use your real name instead of trying to hide your identity. Who is going to gain credibility faster? Someone with the username of BigDaddy23 or John Dalton? By no means should you give out all your personal

information, but offering up what's needed will help people trust you more.

Accept other people's opinions-
Not everything your community members will say will be something you like. Don't start arguments or make trouble because you don't agree with another member. Remember they have a right to their opinion. Also, keep in mind, some of those people could be your customers now or in the future, so their opinions could be helpful to your business.

Follow the rules-
Each site has different rules to follow to use their services, so be sure to follow them. Don't do anything that could get you banned from the site. Trust and credibility can come from someone who knows how to follow the rules. Rule breakers can be seen as a person not to be trusted.

Respect the members-
Don't join a networking site and jump in right away by trying to sell your products or demanding they give you some information. They need to get to know you a little before extending any help. Participate for a little while first and when you establish a bond with the other members, you can start to slowly work your products in.

Always return the favors-
When your community members offer some help to help to you by driving traffic to your site or even purchasing an item from you; you should return that favor by doing something for them. By being a taker and never a giver; you will lose their respect and any chances of getting favors in the future.

Participate in the discussions-
Don't just sign up and sit and read other people's comments. Participate in the discussions. How are people going to get to know you and build rapport

with you if you don't give them something to get to know you with? Also, contribute to the discussion both ways, one way promotional posts get annoying ;)

Social networking sites are transforming the way internet marketing works. Why spend a lot of money trying to advertise your site and get inside information on your target audience, when you can do both, inexpensively, with one of these sites. Some of the biggest names in the internet marketing industry have figured out that their customers like conversation. This is what makes a sale more personal. Reading words on a website is cold and impersonal, and it doesn't give them much to relate to.

Social networking sites will give them the personal touch they need before they exchange their money for your products or services. People tend to buy items from those they have some sort of trust with. The socialization these sites provide enables you to reach out to your customer base so they can see the person behind the business.

Social Networking sites have been around for a while and more of them are popping up all the time. They're not going away anytime soon, so if you want to increase your business; you should get on board.

Craigslist

Craigslist is an internet phenomenon. This classified ad site is huge and your customers use it ! If you are not already familiar with it, get to know www.Craigslist.com because you can profit from it. Sign up for an account (you'll see the link along the left side) so you can easily control your posts.

If you offer a service then check the competition on Craigslist for any good ideas they may be using that you could also make use of. You can post ads in the "services" category that best describes your service. When you start posting, you'll need to choose a category in a city nearest you then fill in the form. A title is mandatory and should be honest but catchy. The location is not required but will help target local users so feel free to mention where in the city you are unless it does not matter. The price is not required but if yours is a special offer then by all means show it. The body of the ad itself is similar to a newspaper classified but you have more space so be precise and descriptive. You'll see and "add/edit images" button so browse to your computer and add a photo of two even if they are just pictures from your website. Craigslist users open ads with photos more often than those without. After you click on continue you can proofread the ad before its posted and edit if needed, then continue and enter the two words or partial words in the Captcha boxes and hit enter and your ad will be live soon (usually within 15 minutes so don't do this at 3am. As there are more readers during business hours than in the early am) and will appear at the top of the category until someone else posts to the same category. Your ad will gradually move down the list and every three days you should sign into your account and delete your ads then repost them so they'll be back atop the category. If you post three different ads (one per day) then you can rotate so that you'll always have a current ad.

If instead of a service you sell a tangible product then you can do the same but in the "for sale" categories. These ads can contain the name of your business as well as links to your website and are important more for the local branding of your company then the sales they may generate directly. Everyone on Craigslist who is looking for a product or service will be aware of your company and its offerings.

MeetUp.com

www.MeetUp.com is a social networking site where people can find other locals who share a common interest. If you search your city and find a group whose interests tie in with your company, join and attend some meetings to see if they are potential customers. You can put up a profile that mentions your service or product and how it can benefit the members as well as meeting them personally and hearing their concerns and issues. Remember that your business is building relationships. If you do not find a group that is aligned with your business you can form one and let current customers know about it and as the group grows your sponsorship of it and participation in it will translate into profits as more people learn about your business and you.

Twitter

It seems Twitter is everywhere. Twitter is a social site where users send short messages (tweets) about something and other users can see them and respond. After you sign up for an account (either in your own name or the business name) you can pay someone a few dollars to customize your Twitter page (I charge $50) for you so that it has the look and feel of your business. Then go to Twitterhood.com and find local twitter users and add them to your list of those you follow (this means those whose Tweets you'll be able to see). Many of them will follow you back. You may also want to follow some of your competitors. Ease your way into the community by reading others posts and when you can, answer questions.
After you are comfortable with the atmosphere you can occasionally mention a sale at your place or a special you are running but don't make every post about your business or you drive customers away. Join conversations and treat it as a wedding reception where you don't discuss business unless the topic is brought up by someone else.

LinkedIn

LinkedIn is a more business oriented social network site where users are encouraged to tell each other about their business as well as help others with their business problems. Here's a useful tip for use with LinkedIn; when you sign up for an account, use either your business name or your own full name in the space labeled "first name" so that in the place labeled "last name" you can put your email address so others can contact you easier than going through LinkedIn's third party email system. Participate in discussions and when you can, answer questions as this can build your status as an authority figure which can only help your bottom line.

All of these social media sites have value and should be utilized.

Now lets move on to website that most interests you...

Your Own !

Getting Your Website

Getting your business website up and running well can be broken down into five distinct parts.

Registering a domain name

Signing up for web hosting

Site creation

On-Page SEO

Off-Page SEO

We'll look at what's involved in each step.

Registering a Domain Name

Domain names, or website names, such as www.GreensboroOnlineMarketing.com or www.Amazon.com are not free. They must be purchased and their ownership renewed periodically. A number of factors come into play when deciding on a domain name for your site. First, it must be available (you can check on the availability of any names at www.InstantDomainSearch.com) and second it should be one that will best suit your purpose. This may mean it should copy your business name, i.e. , BillsWidgetSupply.com or it may mean you'd be better off choosing one that describes the location and type of business, i.e. , DetroitsBestWidgets.com. What would someone who doesn't know of your business type into a search engine in order to find a business like yours ? The answer to that question is often the best domain name you could choose.

Once you've decided on an available domain name for your website you can purchase that name at a number of registrants. I use and recommend GoDaddy.com because a quick search for "GoDaddy promo codes" will bring up many special deals on domain names so my purchase can be less expensive but expect to pay less than $10/yr when you register a domain for five years. No matter where you purchase the domain, the registrant will attempt to sell you other products or services along with it. Other than hosting, most of the add-ons are not requirements but merely extras that you may not need so read the descriptions and if you don't understand something either call the registrant, email me or just skip that option for now.

Signing up for Hosting

Wherever you get the domain name will probably offer to host the site for you at an additional cost. The prices for this service vary widely. Your site must be hosted on someone's reliable, secure server so that all internet users can get to it when they want. This hosting can be had from a reliable company like Hostgator.com for as little as $8 per month and I've seen hosting companies offer hosting for $99 per month so shopping around can mean a big difference over the months and years. (Feel free to contact me for hosting at a flat $100 per YEAR !
Terry@GreensboroOnlineMarketing.com)

Site Creation

The design and creation of a website can be as simple or complex as your imagination. Some elements of it are obvious, some not so much. Your site should be something that says what your business offers to its customers, why it is the best choice for them, where it is located, how they can make a purchase or learn more,etc...

Perhaps you also want them to be able to see a video of how you make your product or what your service will entail, you may want to show photos of satisfied customers along with testimonials, you may want to have a Frequently Asked Questions section if half the calls you field regularly ask the same things about your business. You'll almost certainly want a form where they may email you for information as well as your phone number so they can easily contact you. If there is a common design to both your business cards and your storefront you may wish to incorporate that look.

How big should your site be ?

Your site needs to have a homepage, a sort of front porch entrance to the rest of the site that is both inviting and informative that is easy to navigate and that displays both your company

name and a phone number prominently.
You'll most likely have an "About Us" page that establishes both your expertise and your likeability so potential customers get to know and trust you.A "Contact" page should list every option for contacting you with questions or orders by phone,fax,email,driving directions,etc... A page detailing that you will not abuse the personal information (emails or names) or customers is also common. Each product or service you offer should also have its own page. This allows Google and other search engines to find that product or service when someone is searching specifically for it. For example, you may sell mattresses but someone searching for a Queen size Sealy PosturePedic would rather find your page about that than having to go to your home page and then search again for the size and type they want.

Always make it as easy for the potential customer to purchase as possible.

On-Page SEO

SEO or Search Engine Optimization should be done on each page of your website. Referring to the figure below:

Noting the red numerals along the left margin, **number one** refers to the Title of the page and Google pays attention to it so it should mention your location, your type of service or product and the business name (your keywords).

Number two is the domain name itself which hopefully repeats some of the information from the title tag above. Google also pays attention to this.

Number three is the header or headline of the page which should also cover some of the keywords mentioned above and **number four** is the footer which ought to contain your keywords also.

Google and the other search engines look for these elements when determining what a searcher is looking for so having your keyword present in as many of these as possible is a good thing. Sprinkled throughout the actual content on the page is no doubt mention of these keywords naturally. All these work together to show Google that your site is relevant to anyone seeking your service or product in your city or area.

Again each page of your site should have these elements tweaked to the contents of that page so that when someone searches for "industrial widgets in detroit" they are shown not only your home page but also your pages that deal specifically with industrial widgets. The more of your pages that appear on Google's first page the better. Even if your site is not the no.1 result, if it is three of the next four then that will bring plenty of inquiries and profits !

Off-Page SEO

Any search engine optimization work for your site that is done elsewhere, online or off, falls into this category. You should ensure that current customers know you now have a website and display it on all receipts as well as any advertisements you have. Add the website to your local business listings as well as your Twitter, Facebook, and LinkedIn accounts. When you send out correspondence, your website should be on the letterhead and/or signature line. Any articles you write or Press Releases should also link to the site. Any Craigslist postings, MeetUp groups or Yahoo groups you are a meber of should have links to the site. These links, known as backlinks or one way links, help Google determine the relevance and importance of your site.

In Summary

We've covered several ways that your business can gain exposure, authority, trust and ultimately customers through the internet. The methods in this book are not exclusive to me and this is not an exhaustive compilation, but most of these can be done by anyone for their own business. Some of these you may not have the time or desire to do yourself in which case you can hire someone to do it for you. Check locally or just Google your keywords and see what pages are atop the search engines and hire their online marketers.

Or go to www.GreensboroOnlineMarketing.com and I can help with everything covered here and so much more. There are certainly many techniques not brought up here either due to their complexity or the required learning curve, but effective campaigns often include article marketing, podcasting, video marketing and blogging as well as multiple backlink efforts.

But the information in this book will put you ahead of 90% of small business owners out there and that includes your competition.

So if you haven't already (shame !), get started on dominating your market and becoming the leader in your business locally. Hire a competent web designer and superstar marketer or roll up your sleeves and dig in yourself.

A month after initiating your local business listings and the other techniques send me a testimonial along with your business info for a future book !

Terry@GreensboroOnlineMarketing.com